THE DIG

Dig In • Find the Treasure • Put it on Display

Proverbs • Wisdom Walks
Patrick Schwenk
www.thedigforkids.com

TABLE OF CONTENTS

A Word to Parents 1

About Discipleship 2

About *The Dig* 3

Introduction to Proverbs 4

Section 1: Wisdom Walks 7

   Lesson 1: Wisdom Begins with God 8

   Lesson 1: Wisdom Begins with God 9

   Lesson 3: Wisdom Is Worth It 10

   Lesson 4: Wisdom Requires a Choice 11

Section 2: Wisdom Walks in Words 15

   Lesson 5: Words Belong to God 16

   Lesson 6: Use Your Words to Heal 17

   Lesson 7: Be Careful of Lying Lips 18

   Lesson 8: Be Careful of Gossip 19

   Lesson 9: Your Heart Speaks 20

Section 3: Wisdom Walks in Hard Work 23

   Lesson 10: God Created Work 24

   Lesson 11: Work Hard 25

   Lesson 12: Work Wisely 26

   Lesson 13: Work Honestly 27

Section 4: Wisdom Walks in Friendship 31

Lesson 14: Looking for Good Friends 32

Lesson 15: Better Together 33

Lesson 16: Be a Faithful Friend 34

Lesson 17: Fixing Friendships 35

Section 5: Wisdom Walks in Emotions 39

Lesson 18: Get Control 40

Lesson 19: Godly Fear is Good Fear 41

Lesson 20: Watch Out for Anger 42

Lesson 21: Be Thankful 43

Lesson 22: A Humble Heart 44

Section 6: Wisdom Walks in Family 47

Lesson 23: Honor Your Parents 48

Lesson 24: Be Teachable 49

Lesson 25: A Godly Man 50

Lesson 26: A Godly Woman 51

In Closing 54

About the Author 55

Additional Resources 56

A WORD TO PARENTS

Hello, and welcome to *The Dig*!

I am a pastor, husband, and parent. Currently, my wife and I have four children twelve years old and younger. My wife and I clean up spills, refill drinks, do laundry, cut the grass, serve in ministry, drop kids off, pick kids up, take out the trash, clean the house, do more laundry—you get the point!

Like you, my wife and I wear many hats. One of the greatest joys in my life is being a dad and having the pleasure to be a pastor to my kids. My daughter said to me several years ago, "Dad, I am glad you are a pastor." When I asked her why, she said, "Because you teach us the Bible."

The truth is, every parent should be (and can be) a pastor to his or her children. *The Dig* has been my personal desire and attempt to teach our children the Bible from an early age.

The Apostle Paul makes an interesting comment regarding Timothy's training as a child. In 2 Timothy 3:14-15, Paul says, "But as for you, continue in what you have learned and have firmly believed, knowing from whom you learned it and **how from childhood you have been acquainted with the sacred writings,** which are able to make you wise for salvation through faith in Christ Jesus."

Paul suggests that Timothy was being taught the Bible from a very young age. *The Dig* is an effort to systematically help you as a parent study through different books of the Bible with your children. Out of the experience you create, biblical principles are learned and lived.

The goal, of course, is that our children will fall in love with Jesus as their Savior and grow up to follow Him with all their heart, soul, and strength. I trust that this will be a great resource for you and your family!

In Jesus,

Patrick Schwenk

ABOUT DISCIPLESHIP

Before we get too far into *The Dig*, let's look at a few brief observations about teaching and training our children to be disciples of Jesus.

1. We must have the **RIGHT PICTURE** of who we want our children to be. Close your eyes for a moment and picture your son or daughter when they are 15, 25, or 35 years old. What do they look like? What do they care about? How do they pray? How do they worship? Whom do they love? As Christian parents, if the picture of our children is anything other than a disciple of Jesus, then we are aiming at the wrong target. The goal is to raise children who live, love, and serve like Jesus!

2. We must have the **RIGHT PRIORITIES**. The right picture helps us establish the right priorities. What is important to you as a parent? What do you push your children to get involved in? Why? What does success look like for you as a parent? What does success look like for your child? One of the great joys of being a parent is having the opportunity to raise children who love God. This doesn't happen by accident. It is by God's grace and our own effort to establish godly priorities.

3. We must have the **RIGHT PERSPECTIVE**. It is still God's grace that saves our children and not our best intentions or methods. With this said, keep in mind the following:

Information: Children are oftentimes growing up in American churches and homes less biblically literate than the previous generations. As parents, we need to be reminded of the tremendous responsibility we have to pass on the truth of God's Word.

Impression: The goal is also to leave a positive spiritual impression on the hearts of our children. Our children won't have a pleasant memory if all they remember is Mom or Dad (tired and grouchy) drilling Bible verses into their heads! Taking your child through *The Dig* should be a memorable experience. Best lessons are taught within the context of loving and meaningful relationships.

Imitation: Don't forget that our children listen to us and watch us. As a parent, we must be growing as a disciple of Jesus ourselves. We want to be able to say, as Paul did to the church in Corinth, "Follow me as I follow Christ" (I Corinthians 11:1).

ABOUT THE DIG

Shortly, you will meet a character named Doc. Doc is an experienced Bible scholar and archaeologist who will be your Dig tour guide during each lesson. A typical Dig lesson follows the same pattern consisting of four main parts. Below is a short description of each of these four components.

The Map: Each lesson has a map. The Map tells you and your child where you'll be going in each lesson. It is a short summary of the study ahead.

The Dig: The Dig is the main passage(s) you will be studying. Following each passage will be several questions designed to help conversation and understanding. They are meant to be a guide. You can use them or tweak them to help you talk with your children.

The Treasure: The Treasure is the big idea of the lesson. In a short statement, it is what you want your child to remember from the passage you studied.

The Display: When an archaeologist finds a treasure, they will clean it up and put in on display for everyone to see. This is the basic idea of the Display. It is the application of the Treasure you have found. This is a great opportunity to discuss with your child how he or she can live out the truth of God's Word for everyone to see.

After each section, you will reach **The Oasis.** The Oasis is a chance to review what your child has learned so far. Make it your own and make it fun. A quiz and activity are provided, and you can provide the prize! You'll also notice there are key verses in each section. Memorizing God's Word is a great way to hide Scripture in the heart of your child and also to reinforce what your son or daughter is learning.

Enjoy the adventure!

INTRODUCTION TO PROVERBS

Greetings!

I'm Doc! I've been studying the Bible, history, and archaeology for a long time. I love to learn about God's Word and teach others, too. I am very excited you are joining me on this Bible adventure through some very important topics found in the book of Proverbs.

The Bible uses different styles of writing to communicate God's message. For example, some books of the Bible use stories (narratives) to tell us the history of God's people. Other books contain poetry, laws (or commandments), and even prophecy (information about the future).

The book of Proverbs is known as poetic or wisdom literature. The book of Job, parts of the book of Psalms, Ecclesiastes, and Song of Solomon are all examples of wisdom literature, too.

A proverb is a short, memorable saying that is true. They were written in a style that would help someone easily remember God's important truth to live out. The word "wise" or "wisdom" is used over 125 times throughout the book of Proverbs. These short proverbs are meant to help make you wise! And by wise, I don't mean just smart—I mean someone who lives well. A wise person is someone who has godly knowledge and makes godly choices.

Who is the author?

Solomon wrote the book of Proverbs (Proverbs 1:1, 10:1, 25:1). As you probably remember, Solomon was one of the great kings of Israel. 1 Kings 4:29-35 records for us how God blessed him with great wisdom:

> 29 God gave Solomon wisdom and very great insight, and a breadth of understanding as measureless as the sand on the seashore. 30 Solomon's wisdom was greater than the wisdom of all the men of the East, and greater than all the wisdom of Egypt. 31 He was wiser than any other man, including Ethan the Ezrahite—wiser than Heman,

Calcol and Darda, the sons of Mahol. And his fame spread to all the surrounding nations. 32 He spoke three thousand proverbs and his songs numbered a thousand and five. 33 He described plant life, from the cedar of Lebanon to the hyssop that grows out of walls. He also taught about animals and birds, reptiles and fish. 34 Men of all nations came to listen to Solomon's wisdom, sent by all the kings of the world, who had heard of his wisdom.

What is the purpose of Proverbs?

Throughout this study, you are going to be learning wisdom to help you walk through life in a godly way! Wisdom always requires a choice. These proverbs are meant to help you build godly character. Proverbs was written to help prepare you for the many choices you will face as you walk through life. As we'll see in this study, God wants us to walk in wisdom with our words, our work, our friendships, our emotions, and our family.

Are you ready for an adventure through Proverbs? I am! Let's pray and get ready to check out our first **map**, go on a **dig**, find our **treasure**, and put God's Word on **display**!

Let's dig,

DOC

SECTION 1
WISDOM WALKS

Section 1 consists of four lessons.
These four lessons lay a foundation
for understanding biblical wisdom.

LESSON 1:
WISDOM BEGINS WITH GOD

Key Verse: Proverbs 1:7

The fear of the Lord is the beginning of knowledge; fools despise wisdom and instruction.

The Map:

What do you fear? You might find this surprising, but I fear flying! While I have flown to Israel many times, I still feel afraid every time I step into an airport. But not all fear is bad. In fact, the Bible says that we should have a healthy fear of God. As we'll see in our first lesson, this is where wisdom begins. Let's dig!

The Dig: Proverbs 1:1-7

1. As you read verses 1-6, do you think we are born wise or do we have to become wise?

2. Take a look at verse 7. Where does knowledge and wisdom begin?

3. What does it mean to fear God?

4. What do fools do with wisdom?

The Treasure:

We aren't born wise; we have to become wise! Unfortunately, we don't come into the world automatically living for God. Wouldn't that be great if we did? We have to learn and listen to God so that we can live for God. This listening and learning begins with fearing God—not in a bad way, but in a way that shows we love and respect Him more than anything else!

The Display:

Wisdom begins with whether we really love and respect God. Take some time to write a note to God. Tell Him how much you appreciate Him and let Him know how you desire to listen to His wisdom.

LESSON 2:
WISDOM TAKES WORK

Key Verse: Proverbs 1:7

The fear of the Lord is the beginning of knowledge; fools despise wisdom and instruction.

The Map:

As an archaeologist, I love to search for treasure. Sometimes this is backbreaking work! But with all the hard work that comes with the job, I always find a treasure on a dig. The treasure doesn't come to me; I have to go find the treasure! But the work is always worth it. Finding God's wisdom is the same, so let's start digging!

The Dig: Proverbs 2:1-6

1. Does wisdom come to us or do we have to find it?

2. Write down all the words in these verses that describe an action. Feel free to put these in your own words (For example, in verse 1, we have to "receive" wisdom).

3. Take a look at verse 4. What is wisdom compared to?

4. What does God promise us?

The Treasure:

We have to go searching for wisdom! Just like I have to search for treasure, we have to look, ask, search, and call out for God's wisdom. The promise from God is that we never come up empty. He always gives wisdom when we ask and search for it!

The Display:

Take a moment and read James 1:5. Make a list of where you need God's wisdom the most right now. Maybe it's with your friends, your attitude, words, or relationship with siblings. Begin by writing those down today!

LESSON 3:
WISDOM IS WORTH IT

Key Verse: Proverbs 1:7

The fear of the Lord is the beginning of knowledge; fools despise wisdom and instruction.

The Map:

Have you ever had to work really hard for something? What was it? When I first traveled to Egypt, I had to work really hard to save the money to go. But it sure was worth it! I had the chance to see the pyramids, the Red Sea, and the Nile River for the very first time. In this lesson, we're going to see how searching for wisdom is worth it. Let's dig!

The Dig: Proverbs 2:7-15; Matthew 5:6

1. Write down all of the words that describe what God's wisdom does for us. You may need to read through this passage again carefully.

2. Who does wisdom protect us from?

3. Take a moment and read Matthew 5:6. What does Jesus promise us in this verse when we hunger and thirst for God?

The Treasure:

God's wisdom satisfies us when we seek it! When we believe in Jesus as our Savior, He forgives us and loves us completely. We are saved not because of what we do, but by believing in what Jesus did for us. Our search for God's wisdom protects us and satisfies us. God is worth knowing!

The Display:

Maybe you have friends who are not walking in God's wisdom. Take some time tonight to pray for them. Ask God to help you to be a good example to them.

LESSON 4:
WISDOM REQUIRES A CHOICE

Key Verse: Proverbs 1:7

The fear of the Lord is the beginning of knowledge; fools despise wisdom and instruction.

The Map:

Hiking in the desert requires a lot of choices. High in the mountains, choosing the wrong path can be deadly! Wise hikers know that they should think carefully about their journey, using maps to ensure a safe trip. Walking in wisdom requires daily choices, too. Let's dig!

The Dig: Proverbs 4:1-27

1. Take a minute and look back at verses 11-12. What does wisdom do for us as we walk through life?

2. Read verse 18 again. When you choose to walk in the path of wisdom, what is it like?

3. Take a moment and read verse 19. When you choose not to walk in the path of wisdom, what is it like?

4. What do verses 26-27 say we should do?

The Treasure:

You have to choose to be wise! Your parents can't make the choice for you. Your friends can't make the choice for you. Only you can choose to walk the path of God's wisdom. Each day as you are choosing God's wisdom, you are building godly character that will protect you!

The Display:

Take a few minutes before bedtime tonight and go outside where it is really dark. With your parent, read Proverbs 4:19. Talk about how choosing to ignore God is like walking in darkness.

THE OASIS

Congratulations! You have made it through Section 1! The Oasis is a chance to stop, rest up, and review what you have learned so far on the adventure. During each Oasis, you will be quizzed over the lessons you have already done. Do you think you can remember what you have studied so far? Let's find out!

Review Key Verse: Proverbs 1:7

Take a minute and tell your mom or dad the key verse. Remember, you are not allowed to look!

Review Questions:

1. What is a proverb?

2. What is wisdom?

3. What is the beginning of wisdom?

4. What do we have to do to gain wisdom?

5. Explain what wisdom can do for us.

6. For those who don't walk in wisdom, what is the path like?

7. For those who do walk in wisdom, what is the path like?

OASIS ACTIVITY

"THE FEAR OF THE LORD IS THE BEGINNING OF KNOWLEDGE; FOOLS DESPISE WISDOM AND INSTRUCTION." PROVERBS 1:7

IT IS FOOLISH TO ATTEMPT TO NAVIGATE LIFE WITHOUT FOLLOWING GOD'S INSTRUCTIONS, JUST LIKE IT WOULD BE FOOLISH TO NOT FOLLOW THE DIRECTIONS GIVEN TO NAVIGATE THIS PATH. FOLLOW THE ARROWS AND GET TO THE FINISH.

SECTION 2
WISDOM WALKS IN WORDS

Section 2 consists of five lessons.

In each of these lessons, we'll be exploring how to apply godly wisdom to our words.

LESSON 5:
WORDS BELONG TO GOD

Key Verse: Proverbs 18:21

Death and life are in the power of the tongue.

The Map:

Have you ever wondered where words come from? We use words every single day. What we say and how we say it is incredibly important. Why? Well, because words come from God and have great power. In lesson 5, we're going to learn how God speaks. Let's dig!

The Dig: Genesis 1:1-31

1. Take a minute and count how many times in chapter 1 you read, "And God said."

2. What happens when God speaks?

3. What was the world like before God spoke in Genesis 1? Look at Genesis 1:1-2.

4. Read Genesis 1:26 again. Whose image are we made in?

5. Why is this important when you think about your own words?

The Treasure:

Our words matter! When God speaks, He creates beauty and life. There is amazing power in God's words. We obviously can't use words to create things, but we can use our words to love and encourage other people. When we use our words wisely, we are reflecting who God is!

The Display:

The God of the Bible is a God who speaks! Because we are made by Him and in His image, we have the ability to speak as well. But do we always use our words like we should? Probably not! As a Christian, you can use your words to bless others. Write down the names of three people you want to encourage this week.

LESSON 6:
USE YOUR WORDS TO HEAL

Key Verse: Proverbs 18:21

Death and life are in the power of the tongue.

The Map:

Several years ago, I was leading a tour through parts of Turkey (take a minute and find it on a map). We met a man who invited us into his home for a meal. As we talked, he told us his father didn't use very many words. In fact, he never heard him say, "I love you." In lesson 6, we're going to look at why it's important to use words that heal. Let's dig!

The Dig: Proverbs 18:21; Proverbs 12:18; Ephesians 4:29

1. What kind of power do words have according to Proverbs 18:21?

2. What does it mean that words have the power of death?

3. Take a moment and read Proverbs 12:18 again. What do the words of the wise bring?

4. What are we supposed to be careful of according to Ephesians 4:29?

The Treasure:

Use your words for healing, not hurting! It's easy to get upset and say things we shouldn't. Unwise words can bring further hurt to friends or family. God wants us to be careful of what we say and how we say it. Our words can be used to help hurting people feel God's love.

The Display:

Take a minute and read Ephesians 4:29 again. Write down some practical ways that you can help build other people up with your words. Maybe there are hurting people around you that are waiting for a word or note of encouragement. Maybe you have friends at school that need a compliment. Take some time to write down what you feel like God is asking you to do to help bring healing with your words.

LESSON 7:
BE CAREFUL OF LYING LIPS

Key Verse: Proverbs 18:21

Death and life are in the power of the tongue.

The Map:

Has someone ever lied to you? When someone lies, they are showing that they cannot be trusted. Many times, people who sin by lying can really harm the people they are talking to. In this lesson, we'll see why the wise are careful about whom they listen to. Are you ready to dig?

The Dig: Proverbs 17:4; Proverbs 20:15

1. What is a liar?

2. According to Proverbs 17:4, who do liars listen to?

3. Why is it dangerous to listen to a "mischievous tongue?"

4. What are wise words like according to Proverbs 20:15?

5. Why is it so important to be careful who you listen to

The Treasure:

Lying lips will lead you astray! If you're not careful, liars will lead you down a path, or cause you to make choices that can really hurt you. The wise person is careful of whom they listen to. As we discussed, those who speak wisdom are like expensive jewels. In other words, they are valuable people to have in your life! So be careful of whom you listen to. Choose your friends wisely and make sure lying lips don't lead you astray!

The Display:

Pick a day, or maybe even a week, to carry change in your pocket wherever you go. Remember what Proverbs 20:15 says? Each time you feel the change in your pocket, ask God to help you be careful with your ears and truthful with your tongue!

LESSON 8:
BE CAREFUL OF GOSSIP

Key Verse: Proverbs 18:21

Death and life are in the power of the tongue.

The Map:

People love to talk. Unfortunately, sometimes people can be mean with their words, or even talk behind someone's back. In this lesson, we're going to see what the Bible says about gossip. Have you ever heard that word? Let's take a look at what it means. Let's dig!

The Dig: Proverbs 18:8; Proverbs 31:8-9; 2 Timothy 2:16

1. What do you think it means to gossip?

2. Even though we are Christians, we can still struggle with sin. Like a tasty treat, our sinful hearts can still desire bad things (like gossip). Describe a time when you heard someone talking unkindly about someone else.

3. Read Proverbs 31:8-9. What do these verses say we should do when we hear someone taking about or treating someone else unfairly?

4. Read 2 Timothy 2:16. Why should we try to stay away from "godless chatter" (gossip, lying, unkind words, etc.)?

The Treasure:

Don't be a part of the problem; be a part of the solution! Gossip can be dangerous to you and to others. God doesn't want us to keep quiet when we hear others gossiping. Don't be afraid to stand up and speak up! Use your words to honor God and help others.

The Display:

Take some time to discuss how you would handle friends who are gossiping about other friends. What would you do?

LESSON 9:
YOUR HEART SPEAKS

Key Verse: Proverbs 18:21

Death and life are in the power of the tongue.

The Map:

When I was in fourth grade, I suffered a pretty bad cut on my leg playing baseball. I had to get 15 stitches. Ouch! Before the doctor could fix my leg, he had to clean out the inside of the wound. If he would have just given me stiches, he would have never completely fixed the problem. Our words may come out of our mouth, but they really come from our hearts. Let's dig!

The Dig: Luke 6:43-46

1. Take a look at verse 44 again. How are trees identified?

2. If a tree has bad fruit, what does that say about the tree?

3. How are our words like the fruit of a tree?

4. How do we store up good in our hearts?

The Treasure:

Your heart speaks! Our words say a lot about who we really are on the inside. What kind of words do you usually use? Are they kind, encouraging, truthful, or loving? Or are they mean, dishonest, selfish, or hurtful? As God changes our hearts by His Word, the words that come out of our mouth should be more and more pleasing to Him. Be a tree that is bearing good fruit!

The Display:

Take some time to discuss what kind of words usually come out of your mouth. If you are struggling with the wrong kind of words, spend some time praying and asking God to help you change what you say.

THE OASIS

Congratulations! You have made it through Section 2! The Oasis is a chance to stop, rest up, and review what you have learned so far on the adventure. During each Oasis, you will be quizzed over the lessons you have already done. Do you think you can remember what you have studied so far? Let's find out!

Review Key Verse: Proverbs 18:21

Take a minute and tell your mom or dad the key verse. Remember, you are not allowed to look!

Review Questions:

1. What happens in Genesis 1 when God speaks?

2. Whose image are we made in?

3. Why is it important to be careful of whom you listen to?

4. What does it mean to gossip?

5. How does God want us to use our words?

6. Where do our words really come from?

7. How are our words like the fruit on a tree?

OASIS ACTIVITY

"DEATH AND LIFE ARE IN THE POWER OF THE TONGUE." PROVERBS 18:21

OUR SENTENCES ARE CHAINS OF WORDS WHICH CAN BLESS OTHERS WITH LIFE. IN THE WORD-FIND PUZZLE BELOW THE WORD "LIFE" APPEARS SEVERAL TIMES; EACH TIME YOU FIND IT CIRCLE IT. THEN LOOK AT ITS LETTERS TO FIND THE NEXT EXAMPLE OF "LIFE." THE FIRST TWO ARE DONE FOR YOU. WHEN YOU ARE FINISHED YOU SHOULD HAVE LINKED ALL YOUR "LIFE" WORDS TO THE LAST EXAMPLE IN THE BOTTOM ROW. IF YOU FIND THE WORD "DEATH" CROSS IT OUT. WORDS CAN BE WRITTEN FORWARD, BACKWARDS, UP OR DOWN (NOT DIAGONAL) FOR MORE FUN LOOK BACK IN THE PUZZLE AND FIND THESE WORDS:

PROVERBS	LIPS	UVULA	TONSIL
WISDOM	TEETH	CHEEK	
WORDS	TONGUE	MOUTH	
POWER	GUMS	THROAT	

```
L I F E T H T A E D T H O I C R U B D E A T H B
D C S F H L U V E G D E A T H L H W O R D S P I
E P E I N I H T A E D T H E B P T S T E E T W D
A N B L I F E L A M O I N H I E A S A L U V U E
T O L I F E A E M O U T H T D U E G L M P E V A
H W I F S H T A E D I U C A E G D M E S B T S T
C E F B C A S K R I N H O E A N B T A O R H T H
W R E F I L I F E L I P S D T O L D P S V B R L
H E A T H E R D F U R T H E H T M E B U D K U P
W H T A E D C E I K E F I L V L T A S L I F E R
I S W O T H G A L I F E R I D D S T V I L I F E
S G I C H U N T M O I C H F N E C H L F E K I F
D K S M U G D H S G L K T E L A L I F E G B L I
E W D O A D E A T H N T A F B T I M G O E F I L
A O O L S B R E V O R P E I D H F D L D F L P M
T D M H K M V U L M V S D L I F E E R L I O C E
H E P T O D G C P D E A T H O C V A E V L I F E
L A U A C U A H V E R P R E M R A T P O T S H F
I T P E R T E E T H G B D E A S G H S K M T L I
S H P D G V M E C H T A E D V E N L I F E F I L
N C A M D E N K N P O W E R O R P R I P S E L B N
O S G O U H T A E D R P T G O T K F O D E A T H
T U V D E A T H K G W C H A L I F E R N V E E K
```

SECTION 3
WISDOM WALKS IN HARD WORK

Section 3 consists of four lessons.

In each of these lessons, we'll be exploring
how to apply godly wisdom to our work.

LESSON 10:
GOD CREATED WORK

Key Verse: Proverbs 21:25

The sluggard's cravings will be the death of him, because his hands refuse to work.

The Map:

Have your parents given you work to do around the house? Do you enjoy working? One of my first jobs was delivering newspapers. In this section, we are going to learn a lot about how important work is. Work was God's idea! Let's dig and find out how we are supposed to work wisely.

The Dig: Genesis 2:8–17; 1 Corinthians 10:31

1. Where does God put Adam and Eve to live?

2. What were they supposed to do in the garden? If you need a hint, take a look again at verse 15.

3. God gave Adam and Eve the job of working and taking care of the garden before sin entered the world. What does this say about work? Is it good or bad?

4. Take a moment and read 1 Corinthians 10:31. Who are we supposed to do our work for?

The Treasure:

God made us to work! A lot of people try to get out of working by complaining or having a bad attitude. But God made us to be workers and to enjoy it. Adam and Eve were put in the garden to work and take care of God's creation. It is not an accident that God still wants us to work. The real question is how we choose to work!

The Display:

Take some time and write down how you can help your parents work around the house. Are there jobs that you could help with?

LESSON 11:
WORK HARD

Key Verse: Proverbs 21:25

The sluggard's cravings will be the death of him, because his hands refuse to work.

The Map:

In college, I worked with a friend that I called "Mr. Enough." Why? Because he always did just "enough." It wasn't that he didn't work; he just didn't work very hard! He was always making excuses and complaining. This is NOT how God wants us to work. Let's dig and find out how we are supposed to work wisely!

The Dig: Proverbs 21:25; Proverbs 6:6-11

1. What does the Bible mean by a sluggard?

2. According to Proverbs 21:25, why does the sluggard get in trouble?

3. Take a moment and read Proverbs 6:6-8 again. What is an example of a hard worker to the sluggard?

4. What does the ant do that we are supposed to learn from?

5. Look at Proverbs 6:9-11. What can happen to those who choose to be lazy and not work hard?

The Treasure:

Hard work is meant to protect you, not punish you! Sometimes it doesn't feel too fun to have to work. But being lazy is actually dangerous for our lives. God reminds us that working hard actually helps protect us. When we work hard, we are able to provide for ourselves and for our family as we get older. Those who work hard are wise!

The Display:

Working hard is meant to protect us. Take a few moments and write down what kind of attitude we should have while we are working.

LESSON 12:
WORK WISELY

Key Verse: Proverbs 21:25

The sluggard's cravings will be the death of him, because his hands refuse to work.

The Map:

What do you want to do when you are older? What do you dream about becoming? When I was younger, I used to dream about being lots of different things—a basketball player, teacher, and even a police officer! God has a special plan and purpose for your life. No matter what it is, it will require working hard and working wisely. Let's take a look at our next proverb. Let's dig!

The Dig: Proverbs 12:11; 1 Thessalonians 4:11-12

1. What does it mean to chase fantasies?

2. As you have probably already discussed, a fantasy is an unrealistic dream. Why is this dangerous?

3. What is the promise in verse 11 for the person who works the land?

4. Take a moment and read 1 Thessalonians 4:11-12. How does working hard help you?

The Treasure:

Hard work always pays off! These verses are not saying that God wants everyone to be a farmer. The point God is making in these verses is that no matter what you do, you need to work hard, work smart, and be consistent. The "dreamer" in this verse is someone who is lazy and not motivated to go out and get the job done!

The Display:

Take a moment and discuss with your parent what your attitude is toward work. Do you complain? Do you have to be asked over and over again? Do you do "just enough?" Do you work hard until the job is complete? After talking about your work, ask God to help you work hard and work wisely!

LESSON 13:
WORK HONESTLY

Key Verse: Proverbs 21:25

The sluggard's cravings will be the death of him, because his hands refuse to work.

The Map:

Have you ever been deceived? To be deceived means you were tricked—someone didn't tell you the truth. As an archaeologist, I have gotten used to some stores trying to sell fake artifacts. They are being dishonest or deceptive about their work! In this lesson, we are going to learn how God wants us to work honestly or truthfully. Are you ready to dig?

The Dig: Proverbs 11:18; Proverbs 20:23

1. What does the "wicked" man do in verse 18?

2. What about the honest or righteous worker? What are they promised?

3. Take a moment and read Proverbs 20:23 again. Is God pleased with the worker who is dishonest?

4. What are some examples of how people work dishonestly?

5. What are some examples of how people work honestly?

The Treasure:

Don't just work to get a paycheck; work to please God! The dishonest worker will do whatever he or she thinks is okay to make money. They might lie or cheat to get ahead. The honest worker knows that pleasing God is the first priority! Dishonesty always comes back to hurt you. God promises in these verses that there is a great reward for those that not only work hard, but for those who work honestly.

The Display:

Doing the right thing is not always easy, but it is worth it. Take a moment and write Proverbs 11:18 on a piece of paper. Stick it in your pocket or put it on your mirror as a constant reminder of how God wants you to work!

THE OASIS

Congratulations! You have made it through Section 3! The Oasis is a chance to stop, rest up, and review what you have learned so far on the adventure. During each Oasis, you will be quizzed over the lessons you have already done. Do you think you can remember what you have studied so far? Let's find out!

Review Key Verse: Proverbs 21:25

Take a minute and tell your mom or dad the key verse. Remember, you are not allowed to look!

Review Questions:

1. Where did God place Adam and Eve?

2. Was there work before or after sin entered the world?

3. What is a sluggard?

4. What is the promise for someone who works hard? For help, see Proverbs 12:11.

5. What happens to the person who is a dishonest worker?

6. What is the good or honest worker promised?

7. What is one way you can work hard?

8. What is one example of how you can work with honesty?

OASIS ACTIVITY

"THE SLUGGARD'S CRAVINGS WILL BE THE DEATH OF HIM, BECAUSE HIS HANDS REFUSE TO WORK."

PROVERBS 21:25

THE WORD "SLUGGARD" SOUNDS SIMILAR TO OUR WORD FOR "SLUG." BOTH SLUGGARDS AND SLUGS ARE A NUISANCE AND AVOID WORK. CAN YOU FIND THE 7 SLUGS SLOWING DOWN THE WORKERS IN THE VINEYARD? COLOR THE WHOLE PAGE FOR MORE FUN!

SECTION 4
WISDOM WALKS IN FRIENDSHIP

Section 4 consists of four lessons.

In each of these lessons, we'll be exploring how to apply godly wisdom to our friendships.

LESSON 14:
LOOKING FOR GOOD FRIENDS

Key Verse: Proverbs 20:6

Many claim to have unfailing love, but a faithful person who can find?

The Map:

Have you ever gone searching for something? As an archaeologist, we are always looking for artifacts. Most of the searching is hard. Sometimes we spends hours, weeks, or even months before finding something of worth. In this next section, we are going to explore how finding good friends is hard, but so important. Let's start digging!

The Dig: Proverbs 17:17; Proverbs 12:26

1. What does Proverbs 17:17 say a friend does at all times?

2. What does it mean that a brother (or friend) is born for a time of adversity?

3. Take a moment and read Proverbs 12:26 again. What does this verse say about choosing friends?

4. What happens to them when they choose foolish friends?

The Treasure:

Your friends will shape your future! Who you choose as your friends can either really help you or really hurt you. As we just read, foolish friends have a way of leading us down the wrong path. God desires that we be very wise when looking and choosing our friends.

The Display:

Take some time and write down the qualities or characteristics you want in a friend. In other words, what makes a good friend worth having? Here are a few ideas to get you started:

They love God   Honest   Reliable

LESSON 15:
BETTER TOGETHER

Key Verse: Proverbs 20:6

Many claim to have unfailing love, but a faithful person who can find?

The Map:

Some of my best friends are ones I met while in college and graduate school. God puts the right people in our lives when we need them the most! And guess what? Friends are meant to help each other grow—sharpening and strengthening one another! Let's see how in this next lesson. Let's dig!

The Dig: Proverbs 27:6,17; Ephesians 4:15

1. What does it mean that wounds from a friend can be trusted? Do good friends always tell you want you want to hear?

2. When a friend speaks truth into our lives, sometimes it can hurt. But why is that kind of a friend someone we can trust?

3. Take a moment and read Proverbs 27:17. What does this verse say a good friend should do?

4. What are ways good friends make us better?

5. Take a moment and read Ephesians 4:15. When a friend has to speak truth or challenge us on something, how should they do it?

The Treasure:

We are better together than we are alone! God not only wants us to have friends—He wants us to have good friends. A wise friend is someone who is going to make you better. It might be through their help, a word of truth, encouragement, or even correction. Friends are a gift to one another!

The Display:

One of the best ways you can help other friends is with your encouragement. Take some time and write one of your friends an encouraging note. Include Proverbs 27:17 as a part of your note to them. I am confident it will mean a lot to your friend!

LESSON 16:
BE A FAITHFUL FRIEND

Key Verse: Proverbs 20:6

Many claim to have unfailing love, but a faithful person who can find?

The Map:

I don't like running out of gas—especially in a foreign country! That is exactly what happened to me on one of the last nights during a tour of southern Turkey. Fortunately, several friends who were back at the hotel had their phones near them. You never know when you are going to need a faithful friend to come through for you. In this lesson, we'll be looking at why it is so important to have reliable friends. Let's dig!

The Dig: Proverbs 18:24; Proverbs 20:6; John 15:13

1. What happens to the person with unreliable friends?

2. What does a faithful friend do?

3. Take a moment and read Proverbs 20:6. Why do you think faithful friends are hard to find?

4. Read John 15:13. What kind of love is Jesus talking about in this verse?

The Treasure:

Look for a faithful, not a fair-weather, friend! People that are fair-weather friends are only your friends when things are going well. But the minute you need them, or something bad is going on, they are nowhere to be found! God wants us to not only look for faithful friends, but also to be a faithful friend. Isn't that how God is a friend to us? He has promised to never leave us or forsake us. We can count on Him! That's the kind of friend we should be looking for, and the kind of friend we should be to others.

The Display:

Take a few moments and think of how you can be faithful friend. How are you already being that kind of friend?

LESSON 17:
FIXING FRIENDSHIPS

Key Verse: Proverbs 20:6

Many claim to have unfailing love, but a faithful person who can find?

The Map:

I have a shelf full of artifacts in my office that have been put back together. These broken jugs and oil lamps were once in pieces. But with special care, they have been fixed! In this lesson, we're going to discover how to fix relationships that get broken. Let's dig!

The Dig: Proverbs 20:22; Proverbs 25:21-22; Ephesians 4:32

1. Feelings can get hurt in friendships. What does Proverbs 20:22 say a wise friend won't do when hurt?

2. Take a moment and read Proverbs 25:21-22 again. What do these verses say we should do toward those who aren't friends?

3. Verse 22 is a little hard to understand, but basically it is saying we should repay evil with good. This can actually lead to change in the other person! What are we promised in this verse?

4. Take a moment and read Ephesians 4:32. How are we supposed to treat one another? Even in the best of friendships, there will be times we have to ask for forgiveness, and times we will have to forgive. What does verse 32 say the motivation for forgiving should be?

The Treasure:

You can't fix a friendship without forgiveness! Because all of us still struggle with sin, none of our friendships are perfect. Maybe we say or do something to hurt a friend. Maybe someone hurts us. The answer isn't to just walk away. Because God, in Jesus, forgave us, we should do the same for others when possible. That is not always easy, but with God's help, it is possible!

The Display:

Have you been hurt by a friend? If so, begin praying that God would help you love them and forgive them.

THE OASIS

Congratulations! You have made it through Section 4! The Oasis is a chance to stop, rest up, and review what you have learned so far on the adventure. During each Oasis, you will be quizzed over the lessons you have already done. Do you think you can remember what you have studied so far? Let's find out!

Review Key Verse: Proverbs 20:6

Take a minute and tell your mom or dad the key verse. Remember, you are not allowed to look!

Review Questions:

1. What does a true friend do at all times?

2. What happens when you choose friends foolishly?

3. What does a wise friend do even when they get hurt?

4. What is our motivation for forgiving?

5. What happens to a person with unreliable friends?

6. How do good friends make us better?

7. How should a friend speak truth to another friend?

OASIS ACTIVITY

"MANY CLAIM TO HAVE UNFAILING LOVE, BUT A FAITHFUL PERSON WHO CAN FIND?"
PROVERBS 20:6

TEN FRIENDS WENT TOGETHER TO THE SAME WATER
WELL BUT GOT SEPARATED FROM ONE ANOTHER.
CAN YOU FIND ALL TEN FRIENDS WITH
MATCHING BLACK STRIPED WATER JARS?

SECTION 5
WISDOM WALKS IN EMOTIONS

Section 5 consists of five lessons.

In these lessons we will explore how God wants us to control our emotions in a way that honors Him.

LESSON 18:
GET CONTROL

Key Verse: Proverbs 25:28

Like a city whose walls are broken through is a person who lacks self-control.

The Map:

In the ancient world, people built walls around the city they lived in for protection. If the walls were sturdy, the people were safe. But if a city had no walls, people were in trouble! In this lesson, we are going to learn how self-control is like a wall built to protect you. Let's dig!

The Dig: Proverbs 25:28; Proverbs 10:19; Proverbs 14:16

1. In Proverbs 25:28, what is the person lacking or missing?

2. Take a moment and read Proverbs 10:19. What does the person control in this verse?

3. Read Proverbs 14:16. What does the wise person do?

4. What does the fool do? Is he or she really secure?

The Treasure:

The character you build today will protect you tomorrow! When you choose to control your emotions or actions, you are building a safe and secure wall around your life. Each choice you make is like a brick. How are you building? When you choose self-control, you are building wisely. It's not always easy. The next time you are tempted to lose control, stop and think about what kind of wall you are building!

The Display:

Take a moment and read Galatians 5:22-23. As a Christian, God doesn't want us to just try harder. He gives us His Spirit to help us live different lives. Are you asking for His power and strength? Did you notice that one of the "fruits of the spirit" is self-control? Take a few minutes and write down where you need God's help the most right now.

LESSON 19:
GODLY FEAR IS GOOD FEAR

Key Verse: Proverbs 25:28

Like a city whose walls are broken through is a person who lacks self-control.

The Map:

Traveling to the Middle East can be scary at times. Recently, they had to close down the airport in Tel Aviv due to fighting going on around Israel. Sometimes in life, there is good reason to fear! But other times, we fear the wrong things. In this lesson, we look at what kind of fear is actually good fear. Let's dig!

The Dig: Proverbs 28:1; Proverbs 19:23; Proverbs 3:25

1. What does the wicked person in Proverbs 28:1 do? Do they really have a reason to be afraid? Why or why not?

2. What is the righteous or wise person like? What makes them bold?

3. Take a moment and read Proverbs 19:23. What does the fear of the Lord lead to? What do we experience when we control our fear and trust in God?

4. What does the person in Proverbs 3:25 fear?

The Treasure:

When you fear God more, you fear everything else less! Fearing God means to be in awe of Him. It is to see Him and know that He really is powerful, in control, faithful, and good. When you get scared, you are not only letting fear control you, you are forgetting how big God is. God doesn't want you to live in fear; He wants you to walk by faith!

The Display:

Take a moment and write out Psalm 18:1-2 below. Once you are done writing these verses, circle the words that describe who God is.

LESSON 20:
WATCH OUT FOR ANGER

Key Verse: Proverbs 25:28

Like a city whose walls are broken through is a person who lacks self-control.

The Map:

Do you know someone who can't control their emotions? They are usually not a very fun person to be around! In this lesson, we're going to take a closer look at the wisdom of controlling your anger. Let's dig!

The Dig: Proverbs 16:32; Proverbs 19:11; Romans 12:21

1. Take a moment and read Proverbs 16:32 again. What does this verse say is better than a warrior conquering a city?

2. What does this verse teach about real strength?

3. Take a moment and read Proverbs 19:11. What does wisdom give this person?

4. What does the self-controlled person in this verse do? Read Romans 12:21. What does this verse say we should do instead of getting angry?

The Treasure:

Love is stronger than anger! There will be times in life when a friend, family member, classmate, or teammate lets you down or hurts you. How will you react? Love is always stronger, even if it's not easier. Be careful of letting anger control you. There is great wisdom in walking in love instead of being controlled by your anger!

The Display:

Before you go to bed, try to find some Play-Doh in your house. Take a handful and roll it into a ball. Leave it overnight and take a look at it before you go to bed the following night. You will notice how hard the Play-Doh is. Keep this hard ball of Play-Doh as a reminder of what anger can do to your heart!

LESSON 21:
BE THANKFUL

Key Verse: Proverbs 25:28

Like a city whose walls are broken through is a person who lacks self-control.

The Map:

A lot of Israel is made up of desert. One of my first tour guides in Israel had a Jeep Wrangler. It was the perfect desert vehicle, and just happened to be my favorite vehicle! Instead of being thankful for the car I had, I was envious of the car I didn't have. Envy is wanting what belongs to someone else. In this lesson, we are going to learn about how envy can really steal your thankfulness. Let's dig!

The Dig: Proverbs 14:30; Proverbs 24:19–20; 1 Thessalonians 5:16–18

1. Take a moment and read Proverbs 14:30. What does envy do to you?

2. What does being at peace do for you?

3. Take a moment and read Proverbs 24:19-20. Who are we not to be envious of?

4. Read 1 Thessalonians 5:16-18. What are we to do in all circumstances?

The Treasure:

Envy is the enemy of joy! God wants us to be thankful for what we have, not envious of what we don't have. When we are always looking for more, or the next thing, we are never truly thankful for what we already have. Most importantly, we should always be thankful for who God is and what He has done for us. He is our real source of joy and thankfulness!

The Display:

Take some time tonight and make a list of what you are most thankful for. The next time you are tempted to complain or be envious, pull out your list and look at what you have.

LESSON 22:
A HUMBLE HEART

Key Verse: Proverbs 25:28

Like a city whose walls are broken through is a person who lacks self-control.

The Map:

For part of my schooling, I had to study in Israel under one of the greatest scholars in the world. He had written lots of books and traveled all over the world to speak. The problem is that he thought he was pretty great, too! In this lesson, we are going to look at what the Bible says about pride and humility. Let's dig!

The Dig: Proverbs 8:13; Proverbs 22:4; Proverbs 18:12; Proverbs 29:23; Philippians 2:3-4

1. Take a moment and read Proverbs 8:13. How does God feel about pride?

2. According to Proverbs 22:4, what does humility lead to?

3. Take a moment and read Proverbs 18:12 and Proverbs 29:23. What happens to those who are proud or haughty? What does humility lead to?

4. Read Philippians 2:3-4. How do the humble treat others?

The Treasure:

Humility is thinking of yourself less! Have you ever been around someone who thought they were really important? Or how about someone who thought they were better than everyone else? This is what the Bible calls pride. The problem with prideful people is that they don't realize how big and awesome God is! When we really understand how holy, great, loving, and wise God is, we won't be able to help feeling humble. Humble people think less about themselves and more about loving and serving others.

The Display:

Write down two or three things you can do for a brother, sister, parent or friend this week to humbly serve them.

THE OASIS

Congratulations! You have made it through Section 5! The Oasis is a chance to stop, rest up, and review what you have learned so far on the adventure. During each Oasis, you will be quizzed over the lessons you have already done. Do you think you can remember what you have studied so far? Let's find out!

Review Key Verse: Proverbs 25:28

Take a minute and tell your mom or dad the key verse. Remember, you are not allowed to look!

Review Questions:

1. What did people use to build around their cities?

2. Who does the person who walks in wisdom fear?

3. What is envy?

4. What is one way we can defeat envy?

5. How does God feel about pride?

6. What does the Bible say happens to those who are prideful?

7. What is humility?

8. How do the humble treat other people?

OASIS ACTIVITY

*"LIKE A CITY WHOSE WALLS ARE BROKEN THROUGH
IS A PERSON WHO LACKS SELF-CONTROL."*
PROVERBS 25:28

CAN YOU PROTECT THE CITY BY DRAWING A REPAIRED
WALL WHERE IT WAS BROKEN THROUGH?

SECTION 6
WISDOM WALKS IN FAMILY

Section 6 consists of four lessons.

In these lessons we will explore how God wants us to relate as a family. We'll look at what it looks like to honor parents, how to be teachable, and what kind of man and woman God wants you to be as you grow up.

LESSON 23:
HONOR YOUR PARENTS

Key Verse: Proverbs 23:25

May your father and mother rejoice; may she who gave you birth be joyful!

The Map:

In this lesson, we are going to look at how God wants you to treat your parents. They have an authority given to them by God to love you, lead you, care for you, and protect you. Let's look at how God wants you to honor your parents. Are you ready to dig?

The Dig: Exodus 20:12; Proverbs 15:20; Proverbs 23:25; Ephesians 6:1-3

1. What does Exodus 20:12 say you should do for your parents?

2. Take a moment and read Proverbs 15:20. What does a wise son or daughter bring to his or her parents?

3. According to Proverbs 23:25, what does a wise son or daughter bring to his or her parents?

4. Read Ephesians 6:1-3. What are children commanded to do in these verses?

The Treasure:

Honoring your parents honors God! God has placed your parents in your life for a special reason. They have a great responsibility before God to teach, love, provide, and nurture you. When you choose to honor and respect your parents, you are really honoring and pleasing God. You can honor your parents by how you talk to them, treat them, and by listening to them. Just as you are to listen and obey your parents, your parents are commanded to listen and obey God.

The Display:

How are you already honoring your parents? Take some time tonight to write down a few ways you can do a better job honoring your parents.

LESSON 24:
BE TEACHABLE

Key Verse: Proverbs 23:25

May your father and mother rejoice; may she who gave you birth be joyful!

The Map:

You never stop learning. I thought when I was younger that when I became an adult I would know everything. Boy, was I wrong! Walking in wisdom means we keep learning and always have a teachable heart. Let's take a look at why that is so important. Let's dig!

The Dig: Proverbs 1:8-9; Proverbs 3:11-12

1. What does Proverbs 1:8-9 say a son should do with his father's instruction?

2. What does it say he should not do to his mother's teaching?

3. Take a moment and read Proverbs 3:11-12. What should your attitude be to discipline?

4. According to Proverbs 3:11-12, why does a parent discipline a son or daughter?

The Treasure:

A teachable heart is a wise heart! God has put your parents in your life to help you grow and learn. They are responsible to God in how they love you and lead you. It's not always easy being a parent! Your parents want you to grow up to love and listen to God. When they teach you, correct you, or even discipline you, it is because they love you. So keep a soft, humble, and teachable heart—this is wisdom in God's eyes!

The Display:

Write down how you usually respond to your parent's instruction. Now take a few minutes and write down how you think God wants you to respond when your parents are teaching or correcting you.

LESSON 25:
A GODLY MAN

Key Verse: Proverbs 23:25

May your father and mother rejoice; may she who gave you birth be joyful!

The Map:

What do you want to be like when you grow up? In this lesson, we are going to look at what a godly man looks like. Now, if you are a girl reading this lesson, don't skip it! We're going to study what wisdom looks like for men in this lesson, and then women in the next lesson. God has a plan for who He wants you to become. Let's dig!

The Dig: Proverbs 3:5-6; Proverbs 20:6; Proverbs 24:10; Proverbs 31:8-9; Ephesians 5:1-2

1. What does Proverbs 3:5-6 says a man does?

2. According to Proverbs 20:6, what should be true of a godly man?

3. Take a moment and read Proverbs 24:10 and Proverbs 31:8-9. What do these verses say about being a godly man?

4. Who does a godly man speak up for?

5. Ephesians 5:1-2 gives us the ultimate example to follow. What do these verses say about being a godly man?

The Treasure:

Godly men grow up to be like Jesus! God wants you to grow up to be faithful to Him. His desire is for you to be strong, trustworthy, loving, and obedient to His Word. The world needs men like that! So as you are growing up, make sure you are pursuing who God wants you to be.

The Display:

What is one thing you can start doing right now to help become a strong, trustworthy, loving and obedient godly man someday?

LESSON 26:
A GODLY WOMAN

Key Verse: Proverbs 23:25

May your father and mother rejoice; may she who gave you birth be joyful!

The Map:

Okay, girls, now it is your turn! If you are a boy, don't skip this lesson! In this lesson, we'll look at the kind of character a godly woman has. It's not easy to be a godly man or woman, but there is a great reward for those who seek to please God. Let's take a closer look at what that looks like for girls. Let's dig!

The Dig: Proverbs 31:10-12,17,20-31

1. According to Proverbs 31:10-12, what is true of a godly woman?

2. Read Proverbs 31:17. What does this verse say about a woman who loves and fears God?

3. Take some time and read Proverbs 31:20-31. What do these verses say about the kind of speech a godly woman has?

4. What do these verses say about outward beauty alone? What does a godly woman fear?

5. How is the woman in this passage treated by her husband?

The Treasure:

A godly woman is worth more than rubies! In other words, God is saying that a godly woman is of great worth. She is incredibly valuable to God, her husband, her family, and the world! She is a woman who honors God with her speech, her hard work, and her purity. She is a woman worthy of praise!

The Display:

What is one thing you can start doing right now to help become an honoring, hardworking, pure woman someday?

THE OASIS

Congratulations! You have made it through Section 6! The Oasis is a chance to stop, rest up, and review what you have learned so far on the adventure. During each Oasis, you will be quizzed over the lessons you have already done. Do you think you can remember what you have studied so far? Let's find out!

Review Key Verse: Proverbs 23:25

Take a minute and tell your mom or dad the key verse. Remember, you are not allowed to look!

Review Questions:

1. How does God want children to treat their parents?

2. What is one way a child honors his or her parent?

3. Name at least one character quality of a godly man.

4. Name at least one character quality of a godly woman.

5. Who is the ultimate example of a godly man?

6. Why does a parent discipline his or her child?

7. Who does the godly man speak up for?

8. What kind of beauty does the godly woman pursue?

OASIS ACTIVITY

"MAY YOUR FATHER AND MOTHER REJOICE; MAY SHE WHO GAVE YOU BIRTH BE JOYFUL!"
PROVERBS 23:25

AS YOU GROW IN WISDOM YOUR FAMILY WILL REJOICE. UNSCRAMBLE THE WORDS TO REVEAL MANY OF THE TRAITS WISDOM WILL PRODUCE AS YOU GROW. IF YOU NEED SOME HINTS LOOK AT THE LIST PRINTED UPSIDE DOWN BELOW.

TUFFALIH

KENSDISN

MEBUHL   RETNESLAS

EIATPENC   PUGITHR

STERPISTEN   TDIBNEOE   FUSJOLNSEY

THOGESURI   IFMNDUL   TOECTNETNMN

ENHTSO   LEABHECTA   SONOGDES   NOCLSEFOTRL

ISFANRES   CNEREUNAD   FACUEPEL   UKLAFTNH

PATIENCE   RIGHTEOUS   KINDNESS   HONEST
FAITHFUL   SELF-CONTROL   JOYFULNESS   MINDFUL
TEACHABLE   ENDURANCE   CONTENTMENT   OBEDIENT
THANKFUL   UPRIGHT   FAIRNESS   PEACEFUL
ALERTNESS   HUMBLE   PERSISTENT   GOODNESS

IN CLOSING

Congratulations!

You have finished Proverbs! I hope you continue to enjoy reading and studying the Bible as much as I do. The Bible is not just any normal book. It is God's Word, but it is also God's Story!

The Bible tells us how in the beginning God created the heavens and the Earth. Everything and everyone belongs to Him! God created us to live in a loving friendship and relationship with Him. The bad news is that just like Adam and Eve, our sins separate us from God. But the good news is that because God loves us, He sent us a Savior, Jesus, to rescue us from our sins.

John 3:16 says, "For God so loved the world, that he gave his only Son, that whoever believes in him should not perish but have eternal life." The news is that good! When we believe in Jesus, God forgives us of our sins and gives us everlasting life! As Christians, we do not go through life alone. We know that God loves us and is always with us no matter what happens. And best of all, some day we will be together in Heaven with God. Now that is something to look forward to!

I hope you will continue reading and studying God's Word. But most importantly, I pray that as you learn more about God it will help you to love Him more. He is truly amazing and worth living for!

There is a lot more to dig for, so be sure to check out another Bible adventure soon!

Happy Digging,

DOC

ABOUT THE AUTHOR

Patrick Schwenk is an author, speaker, and pastor. Along with his wife Ruth, they are the creators of For the Family (www.forthefamily.org) and The Better Mom (www.thebettermom. com). They met while attending the Moody Bible Institute in Chicago, Illinois. Pat and his wife have been married for sixteen years and have four children ages five to twelve.

For additional information on parenting and discipleship resources, visit:
www.thedigforkids.com
www.forthefamily.org
www.thebettermom.com

ADDITIONAL RESOURCES:

The Dig—Luke Volume 1

The Dig—Luke Volume 2

The Warrior Weekend

Contact Info:

Facebook: Patrick Schwenk

Twitter: @patrickschwenk

The Dig: www.thedigforkids.com

Email: thedigforkids@gmail.com

Design and Artwork:

Cover Illustration and Oasis Artwork by Steve Miller: www.torchbearerstudios.com

Edited by Jordy Liz Edits: www.jordylizedits.com

44639723R00035

Made in the USA
Lexington, KY
04 September 2015